Marmaduke

DIGS IN!

Marmaduke

DIGS IN!

by
BRAD ANDERSON

tempo
books

GROSSET & DUNLAP
A FILMWAYS COMPANY
Publishers • New York

Marmaduke
Copyright © 1978 United Feature Syndicate, Inc.
All Rights Reserved
Published simultaneously in Canada
ISBN: 0-448-14553-7
Tempo Books is registered in the U.S. Patent Office
A Tempo Books Original
Printed in the United States of America

"Police!! Help!! I'm trapped in a
phone booth at 10th and Emerson!"

"I can always tell when he's crabby about something . . . He brings me only ONE slipper!"

"Tell your mother we'll be late for dinner . . .
He's gotten his second wind!"

"I know this is a silly question, but who can
finish this hamburger?"

"I'll tell you ONE thing . . . There's going to be
a special clause about YOU in next year's
union contract!"

"It's mood music. We play soft, soothing,
quiet music to slow him down
when he's in the house."

"Are you trying to say I've got skinny legs?"

"He doesn't like noise, Luke, so put it
down gently ... easy now ...
real easy ..."

"See, he doesn't like oatmeal either."

"There's nothing in the rule book that says you can
hop over Marmaduke's foot!"

"Anything interesting happen while I took my nap?"

"Marmaduke? I don't see Marmaduke.
You don't see Marmaduke."

"Everyone ready now? Daddy has to catch the 8:15!"

"My African violets just go all to pieces
when Marmaduke barks."

"Boy, he sure took that one hard about
Old Mother Hubbard!"

"He was just going to give me a warning
until you kissed him!"

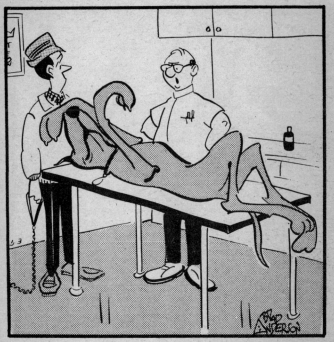

"The biggest hypochondriac I've ever seen."

"All right! But no snoring!"

"That funny smell is cat-nip. Marmaduke's been rolling in it."

"Really! Keep your paws off the wheel
while I'm putting on lipstick!"

"I dread it when he has a good night's sleep!"

"We want to question him about some chewed up parking tickets."

"I made the mistake of patting him on
the head one day . . ."

"Marmaduke got a job babysitting!

"Whatever you do, don't wake him up!"

"Well, I guess I could take the bus
today, Marmaduke."

"Oh no! Marmaduke is trying to move in on us!"

"All of a sudden you're a gourmet?!"

"Why didn't you bark when you saw
that tree coming?"

"The pie is for dinner, and your
name isn't dinner."

"Why is it everytime he and Phil have trouble,
he moves in with us?"

"We can be expecting a call from the
police department, Dottie."

"Don't you think the KIDS should get first
crack at the goodies I bring home?"

"I believe that's MY breakfast you're eating!"

"Mom won't like it. It took her three
weeks to get rid of the last one
you brought home."

"You'd make a great marine sergeant!"

"The night isn't fit for man or beast -- so— wouldn't you know HE'd be out!"

"Move it! Move all of it!"

"He wouldn't be so bad if he didn't snore!"

"Hold still! How do you expect me to get my first
aid certificate if I don't practice!"

"You've done it hundreds of times before!
Marmaduke, open the door!"

"I'm the victim of a squeeze play! I was taking a nap when Marmaduke decided to take one, too!"

"Visiting hours are over now. . . .you'll
have to close the window!"

"No use playing dead. This is the day
for your shot; come on!"

"I said you could have a LICK!"

"When I get to the comics, I'll call you!"

"Talk about ME spoiling the KIDS!"

"Nice try, Marmaduke, but he'll never believe I'm rushing you to the animal hospital."

8-9

"We're having a picnic at Marmaduke's house!"

"OFF! We raced for this chair and
I beat you fair and square!"

"I knew if he ever caught one he wouldn't
know what to do with it!"

"I warned you. . .don't pay him compliments!"

"This is for MY groceries. . . .You get
your own pantry!"

"Bah! Humbug! He's just trying to butter
me up before Christmas!"

"Never mind WHY. . .just take down
all the mistletoe!"

"I've found the culprit, Dottie!"

"I think he wants to bury it!"

"No thanks. . .I'm walking!"

"He loves to help!"

"You may think we spoil him. . .but, believe me,
it's easier when we do!"

"Maybe his water dish is empty."

"I always check here when I can't find Marmaduke!"

"Thanks! . . . I think. . . "

"You're the one who taught him to shake hands!"

"Do you have to participate in EVERYTHING?"

"We're wiped out!"

"When Marmaduke wants to show you something, he won't take no for an answer."

"It's Marmaduke's car. He WON it. And don't ask me why I put HIS name on the raffle ticket."

"Can I borrow Marmaduke? That tough kid
is picking on me!"

"A man's best friend wouldn't steal his chair!"

"Come on in. It's our new clubhouse."

"Just a friend, Marmaduke! One friend!"

"That's no costume--that's REAL!"

"I just can't get him to beg or bark. He just takes!"

"I know you feel sorry for me, Marmaduke, but you don't have to come in every five minutes to tell me."

"I think he likes the sweater but not the booties!"

"Okay, okay. . .I'll get to you!"

"Actually, he BELONGS to the people next
door. . .but he LIVES here!"

"Try sprinkling hair tonic on his head
and yelling 'next'!"

"You shouldn't bark at the construction workers!"

"He wants you to put it in the refrigerator
until he's hungry again!"

"It was a good morning until you opened the shades!"

"You know, some good might come out of
this space age, after all."

"I don't want to be helped across the street.
I'm waiting for a bus."

"This togetherness bit is getting out of hand,
Marmaduke!"

"After I dumped ashes, dust and dirt on the rug, he chased out the salesman before he could demonstrate the vacuum cleaner!"

"I think he had an argument with the Winslows and wants to stay with us tonight!"

"I'm going to count to three...and don't pretend
<u>you</u> can't count!"

"You've got yourself a problem. . .they built their
ant hill right over your buried bone!"

"I said something last week that made him behave.
I wish I could remember what it was."

"Oh, knock it off! I don't need your
grunts and groans!"

"Hold it! I'll fix you something!"

"They've been watching Mommy's soap opera."

"Don't tell me he has a business appointment, too!"

"Breakfast in bed again, you lucky dog!"

"I have a sense of humor--you don't have to point out the joke to me!"

"There's another bad habit he's picked up from you!"

"Now you've done it, Marmaduke! I told you
not to snore too loud!"

"Look out!"

"I need some help getting him out!"

"All set, Marmaduke. . .you can start
rounding up customers!"

"Don't tell me he's just innocently lying there...
he's up to SOMETHING!"

"Guess who didn't notice you put up
the screen door, dear!"

"You have the right idea, Marmaduke, but his clothes come off first."

"I don't know when he's harder to handle: when he's
asleep or when he's awake."

"Hey! Stay out of my dresser drawer!"

"You better have your brakes adjusted!"

"Did you have to growl back at him!"

"No, the roof isn't caving in. He's just munching ice cubes."

"Next time just let me answer the
door alone, Marmaduke!"

"When he finishes, I want to tell you my side of the story."

"Now I suppose you want me to believe that
someone else ate them all up."

12-8

"Notice how he put them just out of reach? When
I go to get them, he'll swipe my chair!"

"But I had my cold first!"

"I thought I was supposed to test drive it!"

"We could have gotten away with running around
the living room but you had to jump on the sofa!"

"Who left the gate open?"

"Better fix Marmaduke an ice pack. He licked
the party glasses dry!"

"NOW what?"

"Maybe he's got more problems than we realized."

"Is there somebody home to say 'Down boy!'?"

"He only looks like he's dozing. . .
he's taking in every word!"

"Now you'll never know how Dracula ends."